Frieze

Frieze

Olga Dermott-Bond

Nine
Arches
Press

Frieze
Olga Dermott-Bond

ISBN: 978-1-913437-80-0
eISBN: 978-1-913437-81-7

Cover artwork: 'Bird Blue', February 2020 © Harriet Horton.
www.harriethorton.com

First published October 2023 by:

Nine Arches Press
Unit 14, Sir Frank Whittle Business Centre,
Great Central Way, Rugby.
CV21 3XH
United Kingdom

www.ninearchespress.com

Printed in the United Kingdom on recycled paper by Imprint Digital.

Nine Arches Press is supported using public funding
by Arts Council England.

Supported using public funding by
**ARTS COUNCIL
ENGLAND**

For Oliver and Clemency

Contents

'She stood at his
burnt windows
until she saw herself
answered in their dark,
the way glass gets
blacked at night
in a lighted room.'

'Maroon, Over Black on Red'
 – Robin Robertson

Silent conversation

The first time we texted, I was standing
next to a dead girl. I had been staring

at her skeleton, seeing how copper had seeped
through soil to paint a belated metamorphosis,

as if peacock feathers and forget-me-nots
had been steeped inside her pelvis, hips.

Time plays interesting tricks; I didn't know
we would exhume bodies of light together,

that you were the one who was going to
uncover my bones, make them a tiny bit

beautiful, over and over, let me lay out
my regrets, unearth blue sky under my feet.

I studied the cathedral ruin of her ribs,
a leaking roof for a heart long-since

crawled through and vanished.
Our silent conversation thrummed

under my fingers, still years away
from your voice, our first touch.

God was so small and inside me then

After 'Annunciation 2: After Fra Angelico from the brass tacks' by David Hockney

God was so small and inside me then, weeks
before I would feel the first flutter, months

before his fist or elbow would gargoyle itself
under my ribs. *We'd better sit down,* the angel said –

quite serious – as if he had forgotten about his wings
spreading behind him like sugared light. We leaned

into each other, me perching on a kitchen stool, edges
of the house cut clean away. In the painting we look

like we're on a merry-go-round, the water full
of pink flowers, but I do remember a blue wall stretching

away so quickly, bright shock, full of slow motion
and split seconds and empty speech bubbles. Gabriel bent

almost in apology – he knew he'd had the easy job.
There I was, fretting already about what to tell Joseph

and my dad, picturing myself trying to explain that things
don't always happen in the right order. We definitely

didn't have haloes then, just bright space around our heads.

We don't need infinity

Zvezda space suit model number KV-2 No 167 used by Helen Sharman

Earth-slight and beautiful, she climbed
inside me, past every seam that was made

for her; how she gazed through
my eyes, how we made continents disappear

by moving her thumb a little to the right.
For seven nights her breath fluttered

against my glass cheek, a mechanical
butterfly. Now, I wait for her bed

to tangle itself into a love knot, up and up and up
out the window, shedding clothes

as I steal an old rocket to make it sing
so she will meet me, naked, our milk-and-stars

folklore shaped around us, the curve
of her spine against me. I will gather

her to me like a wedding dress, bury
my face in a crush of silk, let pins

and needles of days and years fall
to the floor that we will never need to walk

over, turning bright cartwheels in our orbit.

Losing Galileo

I like to imagine Galileo,
his heart swinging like
a chandelier, watching

the stones free-fall, this
tiny world growing larger
with each thought. I like to

imagine an outline
of a new idea sending the earth
spinning round the sun,

I like to imagine him
turning a Tuscan night sky
over in his hand, high up

in the leaning tower. I like
to imagine his name as a poem
folded inside itself, Galileo

Galilei – *but yet it moves* –
400 hundred years on, someone
voted to pack up constellations

of people, unscrew each lightbulb
star, dismantle those tin-foiled
friendly ghosts that float above

telling us where we are inside
our flickering darkness. I hate
to imagine how they will wink

in someone else's back garden,
while we, dull as pebbles, will
lie at the bottom of night's pitch.

Stasis from misunderstanding.
A country in terminal velocity.
Without Galileo, without others

we are only a clouded thought-
experiment that can't imagine
anything better than this.

Mouse

An almond shelled and cleaned,
thumb-perfect. Twitching is not

a possibility. Pinned down beneath
surprisingly pink feet, it can't ever

turn to see
the albino peacock struck beside it.

Hot throb of fine grease when I place
my hand against the glass – beneath

fursoft, skinsoft, its insides taken
out, ribs arranged like a toast rack

in a Victorian doll's house. I want
and don't want to pick it up, roll

it over to see stitches. I stare at
the iron will of this vermin, this

beauty, black eyes brimming with
someone else's tears. The creep

of a thing that thinks it's still alive –

Ophelia's head is finished

"I am getting on slowly, but I hope surely, Ophelia's head is finished…"
– Millais' letter to Martha Coombe, March 6th 1852

A body lit by oil lamp cannot last. Another
day of wintery bathwater contracts each breath,
her blood-tide shallower that it should be.

She knows that he drew the riverbank first –
studied dogwood, willow root, grass-tilt;
knows she's unready to be arranged in the lake.

He has learnt the lines of her neck like prayer.
Slack-jawed, on her back, she studies distant
stars on the ceiling, feels the clasp of her dress

turning to rust on her spine, each seam nettling
her skin. Her body is a book, stained satin folding
and fretting chapters between her thighs.

An agony of stillness. Her wrists are mottled stiff
holding her palms upwards; she can't imagine
these half-wilted peonies once belonged to her.

She longs to be resurrected, wants to fill an empty
space with her own flowers, tries to stop shaking,
her hands holding nothing but creaking, cutting air.

The rest is silence

I'm not in school the day you finish
(I can't remember why). A reversal
from the norm: you missed most of *Hamlet*, Danish
Tragedy remained untouched. Your trouble
tied to the ghost of your dad (an irony
you would note). Your poems about his last calls,
the drink, the lies, his death. Your honesty
peeled back edges of the library walls,
those astounding words you could knit over
jammy dodgers in a lunch break. No plea
would ever make you write them up after,
as each lost week dared you to be or not to be.

You crochet a flower, leave it on my desk.
Such talent. Such damage. No chance of rest.

M25 / turning

A white horse on hard shoulder / galloping hard / beside fields of traffic
    fluency of sweat in his flanks / sun's zoetrope / flickering through
winter trees / thin as paper / inside the spill / of its shadow /
I am turned a curious girl / my car suddenly / an attic in an old house /
staring / at this creature / through a spinning daedalum / thinking
I must be the one / making him run / veined and sinewed
        like this / like this / like this /

Sanctuary

So tired from running
where I started
my heart
inside my hand.
small hours are turned
So tired from running
worn steps
past high hedges
So tired from running
long-forgotten notes
kneel inside choruses
feel my pulse again
dusty catechisms
this stained glass of sound

I find myself back
each field a neglected republic
craving a map that folds easily
When sleep won't come
into tiny electric fences
I need to retrace
through old roads
full of Sunday song
I want to thread
back together
clean as marble
as a chanting psalm
flicker across closed eyes
my sanctuary

flower press

they had unscrewed the weight of a wooden press

lifted layer after layer of cardboard stiff as sermons

                           until they found you

peeled you so carefully from   the brown paper

that had held you fast   laid you out in the open

                        for one more day

all your colours preserved   blue jeans chestnut hair

deep veins rich of you   all halted at once

               beautiful hands

arranged like perfectly rhymed verses   bluebell skin

pale arms   thin stamens a child could draw

                  and meet a smiling flowery face

stained glass red   set darkening on your darjeeling

tea-leaf lips   your eye makeup set differently

                  to how you would like it

a careful outline of yourself   a body following

its familiar indelible pattern   like it almost remembered

                  what it once could do

Outrunning the dark

A retelling of the myth of the Irish Goddess, Macha

Undressed

Macha arrives in the shape of a woman from the underworld

An undressed cry moved like mist
towards her, a disquiet that flayed night air,
fields splayed by this purple-scented call.

A vixen stood: light and deft, seeming
too slight to have made her yearning known
with a din that could tilt the moon.

A goddess stood: shivering, stretched
and keening in her newness, wrapping herself
in the skin of this creature's pitch.

She knew then she would have to be silent,
wait until deep-dark, find a language that could drift
somewhere between despair and certainty –

only a woman now.

Skiffs and skitters
Without speaking, Macha becomes the wife of Cruinnuic

when I first arrived he waited for me to speak   birdsong blistered
my silence   leaving   raw skin of morning peeled back   cherry
trees braced between us   without talking   each glitter of rain on
the roof spoke for me   bright skiffs   skitters of it   distracting
him from my strangeness   whittling my body finer   under
whistling slate   quiet held our days together   spaces in a
spider's web   as if words would turn truth   from silk to
sticky ropes   twist tree roots   fade photographs to ghosts.

Unfurling
Macha can run stronger and faster than horses

My face feathered in grey
I clear the grate early,

hold my breath, like I do
on nights when he reaches

across to touch me
her clothes still folded

in bedroom drawers.

        My face painted silver
        with moonlight, I wait

        to outrun this dark,
        slip off those black boots

        his first wife wore, unfurl
        my feet against wet earth

        run silent as owl-wing run
        my blood-tide rising run

        muscle chasing great swathes
        of fields drunk with rain –

        horses rooted as I fly.

Quieting

Macha becomes pregnant with twins

Back door wide open, I sometimes take a minute
to sit in the long-shadowed sun, everything ticking
and slowing, stone wall at my back cradling me warm.

Catching sudden quince-light as it blooms and falls
on the blackthorn is a trick I have learned here; a golden rope
is thrown across my face, while on the other side of the wall

mice sleep inside an old piano, curled around wires,
creatures that can make any corner home. In the kitchen
last year's apples bake in the oven, bruised-flesh-tender,

holding shape and sweetness for just a little longer. I feel an ache
bloom inside me. On this side of the earth's skin, life opens
like a mustard seed: hot, sharp, and all at once.

Dark earth
Macha outruns the king's horses, goes into early labour
and dies giving birth to twins

ferocious dream –
she sees her children swimming inside
a great glow of undulating glass,
blue glaze of umbilical cord fused
so close to head to curling foot,
misshapen mother of pearl
blood-kissed continent –

it takes only the lightest touch
to break the charm, for their squall
      to stutter to starlight

her blood seeps and empties, ferns turning
the earth a dark map beneath her,
curses burn and rise –

Axe

17th century axe, used for executing criminals, St Andrews Museum, Fife

Such a simple word. Brutal to begin, quick
to end. Glad of the distance between us,

I study it. A ship run aground in a glass case,
its blade narrowing beautifully to a curved keel.

Then the handle, heavy as a church pew, wood worn
in two places from practised hands of a headsman.

I picture a neck exposed, pink sinews propped
like a stick of snapped rhubarb gleaming with sugar

beads for a few seconds, before boards darken,
splinters stained again with a body spilled over.

I study it, the opposite of a lung or a bicycle
or a wildflower, and am reminded of the wail

of a child being left by her mother. A front door closing
as a silvered edge. An unchartered place called severance.

Some things are buried too deep to come out quietly

The dentist removed it
there and then

tackled it with one foot
on the bench, plyers bending,

shoulders straining exquisitely
in his white shirt.

My pain had been turned off,
so sound was the lake I swam in

blood turned up full volume
bulging suction and gurgle, tides of saliva.

Numb-faced and blue-bruised,
I carried my ancient monster home

roots like a viaduct, in the silent hollow
of the afternoon.

Awaiting trial

An electromagnetic field painted a picture
of someone's lungs. That much I understand.

I look past ribs, sepia sad-clowned mouths,
to an eddy of dust rising. Guernica. If I turn

my head one way it grows into a forest, shrinking
mutilated silver into oblique night: tilt left,

it becomes a cathedral ceiling, my cold panic echoes
in this unfamiliar vault, while I search, search

for each hymned black mottle: I want to call out
but the name shrinks inside a line, inside a word,

inside a letter. Try again: I position posteroanterior
and lateral like old fools, Hamm and Clov, fix

their drooping shoulders into a grimace. I squint
for a clue of composition, waiting for them to whisper

a story of what they are hiding, clusters of cells
in syllabary. I have been standing here too long

begging this lunged Meryon to tell me what it means.
Behind me, branches groan with patients' lists,

waiting for their trial, before calling, always calling
my name.

Yellow

When I was a child, I worried
that when my mum went to work
in her yellow car something bad
would happen and she'd never

come back and I wouldn't ever feel
anything yellow again. One time
they tricked me at Nursery, hands
painted bright as two stupid daffodils –

I looked up from the page and she was
gone. Fear spilled like cold sun, impossible
to separate from the swirling water caught
in jam jars, bright honey trapped behind glass.

You were to me

a scientist, who, when I was sick wrapped me
in an old cardigan and aspirin, then took a swab
of my throat, growing bacteria in a petri dish
in the hot press so I saw the reasons, tiny jellyfish,
behind my hot shivers. You were to me a trapeze artist
in sensible shoes who claimed no imagination, no interest
in how ideas could swing glittering above my head
when I flew to catch them. You were to me a Bible,
a guilt-abacus, a great ball of string, a suitcase, sinew.
You were to me a bone collector, your own childhood
rattling in jars in a stammering pantry, trying so hard
to speak. You were to me sandwiches wrapped
in greaseproof paper, all of yourself given away
in hungry parts. You were to me a medicine
of bread and jam, saucepans rattling maternal heat,
oblivious to my 5, 6, 7 melting, like snow from a ditch.

Milk bottle

My mum is standing at the kitchen sink
pressing the silver coin down so carefully

with her left thumb, a dented heart that beats
two days, until it joins the pretend pennies

scattered on the window sill. Above me,
the fat-rimmed lip of the bottle; I can almost

touch the frilly collar of cream that my sister
drinks. My job: to take the empties. I dare

to carry them one-handed, letting their bodies
reverberate, a juddery hollow of sound curling

through my fingers and sliding into their open
throats. I have been taught not to answer back,

not to question the world of empty men,
tight-necked, stout-shouldered. When I reach

the front door, I silence them with a rolled-up
scroll, filled with my very best handwriting.

Chardin's woman

I am Chardin's woman / Edged in reflected light /
Hardened by / The need to be ordinary
– Eavan Boland, 'Self portrait on a summer evening'

The walls are always the colour of dried blood
in his paintings. Handmaids, governesses, girls,

all ruled by that same dark interior that seems
to beset them. There must be a high window

and sun somewhere else, but the beauty of every
dead thing absorbs the little light that falls.

The young kitchen maid pauses, knife resting
in her right hand, staring into the distance.

That hard-backed chair. Beyond her gaze,
these are the narrow rooms we live in yet,

caught in borrowed amber at our kitchen sink
every night, listening to the tightening knots

of years as we wash up, our still lives turning
out the same, ceilings darkening with feathered

moss, blunted hands cupped like empty nests
as we wash our faces, the shape of devotion.

my heart

is a wasp's nest
built slowly in secret
before you realised

i have chewed up all the love
letters I have never written
to you   here   my heart is this

small grey hollowed lightness
that no-one wants near
but now it's too late to hide
from its papery shape

listen to it –
humming with devotion

morning prayer

ruth's hallway is shrunk sacred when her mum gathers us in to
pray   suddenly our arms round each other in a circle of coats
and schoolbags   heads bent i try to hide my surprise as her lilac
voice talks to God as if he is a kind policeman *I ask you, Lord, to*
keep all the wee children safe before pleading for *The Lord Jesus to*
save them from their wickedness   her grip is surprisingly strong no
t.v.   make up   bad books (my house is for that)   as we walk to
school i don't feel any different and Miss Cartmill still can't write
her name straight on the board   under the desks ruth and i read
Sweet Valley High *Heart Breaker   Dangerous Love   All Night Long*
all day i think of her mum's devotion of one-way conversation as
she washes up   giving thanks for His Great Mercy   all mopped
up before half past three

Spin the bottle

I was both meteor and desert sand,
once the vodka bottle had pointed
to me. There was so much I didn't

know – how to kiss a boy, where
Libya was on the map of the world.
Someone's birthday; dressed up

in my sister's make-up, scoop neck
and White Musk. I don't remember
whose house it was, but recall

my stomach marble-tight with fear,
a boy with glasses, who had done this before.
I shut my eyes early, tried not to think

of everyone else waiting cross-legged
for their turn, that head-tilt spinning me
into moldavite, ghost of this new heat.

Valentine's weekend in ~~Paris~~ Rushall

Instead of writing his theology essay,
Eddie made a sign for the M6.

Roadside hopefuls, we stuck out
our thumbs, flayed by fumes and grit,

sprayed with petrol rain. *St Andrews,*
Cupar, Glenrothes, Glasgow; we inched

our way to his mum's house, kissed
in the shallow harbour of every layby

until a little lopsided van parted water
on the hard shoulder, an unlikely Moses

who rattled and chattered and juddered
at fifty miles an hour, all the way to Walsall.

It was first love, first time eating Balti
from a silver bowl, its hammered heart singing

with coriander, listening to him playing
jazz on his old piano, lying in the spare bed

waiting for him to gather me close, closer,
hitchhiking to the moon and farthest stars.

Cutting back the roses

As soon as I spot Dad outside my kitchen window I put the kettle on. He is holding his favourite pair of secateurs, their curved beak of black weighted, ready. It makes sense. Since he has been dead the thing he has missed most is the stubborn stem of a rose that needs cutting back. He has wanted to feel the firm grip of two pieces of metal, that clenched pressure on green bone. His hands are scratched with brutal verbs of thorn-tear, but he is almost through. He takes such pleasure in helping me, cutting down these beauties that want only to live. I will go out and help him, I think, pick up the sparrow lightness of tangled ends, pulled away from today and every other September. Before I can knock the window, he is gone. The overgrown briars sway in silent ululation against the steamed glass.

Tapetum lucidum

I know why ghosts were invented –
to exorcise this feeling of kissing
a dead man's cheek. Beyond blood-

still, freeze-frame of a wave
receding from a shrivel of pebbles.
A silent film of himself dressed

in his best suit. His face an attic,
the undertaker can't get the eaves
of his mouth right. Veered memory

of that last phone call already reflected
back at me strangely. The sound of his
voice lost, sprung into dark hedges.

Five sleeps till Christmas!

Winter light is the same colour as his skin.
We sit next to his corpse, drinking a cup of tea

the nurse brought us. Outside the Mater
low December sky sinks down until feathers

of rain flit grey across the window.
Ash in my mouth, I stare at motes eddying

through half-pulled blinds. A whiteboard
exclaims, *"Five sleeps till Christmas!"*

It's too early to draw the outline of this bad
beginning, or to know where grief will fall:

I begin to scrub, edges of loss spreading
like a bloodstain, further out across the floor.

Strange creatures

For Florence Buchanan 1867 - 1931

She has learnt to pay a different kind
of attention, devoted a life to strange creatures

such as *Squilla mantis*. A name-prayer.

She has studied each part of her: drawn
her naked armour, turned her over

scrutinised this hand-span of softest flesh
jewelled in pearly shell. A body carved

from millions of years. It is lonely work
but think how this silent creature can bury

herself, bide her time, withstand almost

any pressure, wear a wedding dress
men will want to discard before they eat her.

Somewhere over the rainbow

Once the house had been painted, but the sun blistered the paint and the rains washed it away, and now the house was as dull and gray as everything else. When Aunt Em came there to live she was a young, pretty wife. The sun and wind had changed her, too.
– Chapter 1: Cyclone, *The Wizard of Oz*

Dorothy wants me to be her mother
but my bones don't stir to kindness

the way they used to. I plait her hair,
lift my cheek to receive an orphan's kiss

then bury her impatience in the back yard.
Prairies flatline; no stone walls or hills

to hold me. In the dry months I crave
the hum of rain on a tin roof, dream

of our farm floating in the shallows,
but when storms come each drop hurts,

the earth pitted with bitter apple pips.
I set rabbit traps, water down the soup

while clouds push another reluctant
afternoon into the dry well of evening.

kintsugi

the shards of the broken object

gold dust of rain scatters in front of the streetlight outside

are assembled

all other fragments of her fall away

one by one, cleaned and glued

he traces his finger over her open lips

then sanded so metal powder mingles

kisses her with his gentle mouth

intimately with the rich lacquer

it is late and cold in the car but she stays longer

giving the illusion of flowing metal

this is the beginning of her breaking

in all its brilliance

painfully apart

Hare

night full of running,
half-shadowed under winter's
tarnished moon. Dark fields

full of cracked mirrors
glance at her slender bones, face,
catching a fragment

of silver, filled with
heather, willow, thyme –
storm-body breaking

fast, scudding away,
spilling past hard promises
no man ever keeps.

Dead bird

A Golden Shovel

'You say it's only a paper moon
Hanging over a cardboard sea…'
– Harburg and Rose

I carried a dead bird for you in my mouth, waited for you
to collect it from the kitchen floor. *Say you like it, say*
you are going to keep it safe, say it is all you need, say it's
all you ever wanted. I never saw you sweep bodies away; only
the next morning, and then the next, your hands were empty as a
magic trick. Still, I hunted every night, clawed trees to paper
for you *for us, brought you fresh mice, the last owl-hoot, a new moon* –
I didn't know I had been tamed, collared – held or hanging –
my hunger splaying through starved branches like winter light over
hard ground. *Say a kind word, give me back one of my lives, feed me a*
wild lie. It's cold out here. I scratch your backdoor to damp cardboard,
ignore the black windows, howl for you to return, to hold me like the sea.

Possession

"In less than a fortnight I had completed an ivory
miniature of an imaginary Blanche Ingram"
– Charlotte Bronte, *Jane Eyre*

I create her to possess what I cannot have
carve the shape of lips that will seek
his mouth. Every day I invent another piece

of her perfection that he must love –
imagine her collarbone, neck, invent
each cruelty of her beauty, study what I am not.

An undressing of envy and silence, I sit
for hours bent over her profile, crafting
skin to alabaster, walking the long miles

inside myself, treading damp earth down
so nothing will grow. Her tendrilled cheeks
spring as I suffocate myself, pushing parts

beneath stones, my heart shrinking
to a bird skull, hoping I will forget where
it is buried. Each day I shudder towards

the punishment of Grecian neck, labour
over that milky flower in her hair
deepen the gaze that flames his desire

concentrate until blood's metallic song
springs in my mouth.
I catch my reflection in the window –

pale plainness flecked with rain.
On this side, my hands' timidity. Outside,
unbidden wildness hovering beyond the trees.

Personal Touch no. 429

When I get home from work I realise
that the new colour in the living room
is all wrong and also, that I may never
have sex again. In the tin it looked

totally different but now it's all over
the walls, the corners seem oyster pink
and I think about the impossibility
of a tilting, restless kiss on my neck.

Three walls need fixing now. I stand
beside the sofa huddled in the middle,
my skin covered in dust sheets and
can't believe no one will ever undress

me again, one button, slow, after another.
There's nowhere to sit and it's too late
for natural light. I'm crushed by ghost-
headlights that pass through me,

the curtainless windows lit up hugely
for a second or two. Still standing four
shades off, I text the painter. Tell him
I've made a mistake. He tells me not

to worry, that I can have anything I want.

Bury her softly

The lady in the hospital bed opposite doesn't have visitors. She is a bird caught in a cat's mouth, her body a helpless offering, hair stranded damp against her skull. Her skin is the colour of milk, poured into a blue plastic jug. When she sleeps the inside of her mouth drops pink, a fledgling waiting for its next meal, whilst her bones dwindle beneath sheets. I find myself thinking it would be a kindness to wrap her gently in a hanky, carry her home in my pocket, bury her softly at the bottom of the garden, wet and expectant with spring.

Taming the wolf (once upon a time)

A Golden Shovel

The wolf, disarmed of ferocity, is now pillowed in the lady's lap.
– Edward Jenner, *An inquiry into the causes and effects of the variole vaccine, 1798*

Like a penny taken from the jar, a day was lost, and then the
next, until weeks were hollow, covered in dust-quiet. A wolf
came hungry for our flesh; our frail bodies disarmed
so easily. An old man told us not to be afraid, but we knew of
his lies, so the village closed its curtains and prayed with the ferocity
of a child kneeling by his bed. More wolves came. I asked, "Is
anyone going to rescue us?" We were lost to dreams that were filled now
with burning forests. The Wolves crept into bedrooms, savaged us in pillowed
sleep, the sky shrivelling, until one day trees shook and whispered in
secret that a cure was coming, that it lay in us and our blood, in the
dark magic tinier than ground-up bones. An apothecary arrived, gentle as a lady's
smile and saved us; from that day each wolf was tamed, a sleeping dog in our lap.

Sonnet of swimming parts

Human body parts 'pile up' in NHS waste backlog
– BBC News, 4th October

This is a love poem. These body parts
don't know they were meant to be burnt long
ago; don't know an oozing of black hearts
that swim out of plastic bags is so wrong.
Don't know the kiss between elbows and scooped-
out intestines – once punctured tyres – now round
with bacteria, bright as jewels hooped
through dismembered Havisham hands, sounds
grotesque when the radio tells us.
A mourning of ankles, appendices, hurt,
waltzing in darkness of this second chance;
a putrid opera, a wake in reverse.
Tendrils of skin float, odd fish in the depths,
discs brush against fingers, longing to be kept.

Yellow Penguin

Strange pale penguin: rare yellow and white bird
discovered among king penguins in Atlantic
– The Guardian, 25th February, 2021

Instead of black wellies or waders
he is dressed in ballet pumps
and a dazzling cravat, overdressed
for the occasion of the Antarctic.

A fragile daisy who needs the cold
to bloom, his round belly is spilled
with a surprise of yolk, then custard,
smoothing to primrose, then snow –

The others are dressed in leather,
have inherited thick skin, deep tread,
yet his sides are slippery with oyster-
light, a gorgeous hiccup

                    in the genetic loop.

I can only watch while the glacier inside
my daughter calves into something even
more extraordinary, bright – I want
to tell her that one distant day somebody

will discover the exotic creature they are,
no need to hide underneath a black hoodie;
how they'll glow then, in their thin-skinned
difference,

          exactly how he was hatched.

Excision and Eidolon

I had signed consent, but woke up
with my mouth made of Barbie doll,
lower quarter turned plastic –

it took over a decade to get some
feeling back; pins and needles
when I bit my lip, and still,

a ghost floats through the walls
of my lipstick, my baby daughter's
cheek turned strange, like horse hair.

I fumble my fingertips over
my mouth, sense the invisible
boundary between human,

polymer. The breaking of my jaw
was the easy part, but I've learned
to love the three-quarter kisses

that linger between us –
like the faint, pale crackle
of rhubarb growing in the dark.

Aftersun

Space-travelling light has tangled too deep,
entered your body, turned cool-water skin
into a forge; each shoulder blade crackles, creeps
with red knife's edge. You don't blame me
for the constellations across your back
while I try to balance aftersun, a watery
excuse on your shoulders, where swimsuit straps
measure litmus pink, summer-acid cruelty.

You want me to lie beside you through
this white-hot fury: I promise you next time
we'll be more careful, but there's nothing I can do
to unblemish this. The high-wire birds sing
against night's dry bones, lamenting, as one
telling me it's too late, the damage done.

Silk

After 'Lady with a parasol, Madame Monet and her son' by Claude Monet

Lately, I have realised how
I need to piece tiny flecks
of colour together to make a word –

sentences spill and dissipate
like pollen across an open field,
wildflower-vowels skim elsewhere

instead of landing purple and red
at my feet. There is no such thing
as a straight line of sound anymore,

bones are wind-caught, ribboned,
birdsong half-sung, thickening
rain-thrum a distant uncertainty –

when a child speaks to me, cloud
and shadow are crosslit by a careless
sun. Lately, I have realised how spoken

language is like a woman's twisting
body, spine and muscle caught
beneath layers of white rustling silk.

Wardrobe

'I can always go back if something goes wrong'
– Lucy, *The Lion, the Witch and the Wardrobe*

I used to think love would fall like snow –
the hush of it, days like Christmas cards
with fat robins on the front. I used to think

I knew you, laid on my back, made blurred
angels with each confession. After you left
I used to sleep in the back of the wardrobe,

wrapped in a fur-coat smell of boiled sweets,
moth-shadow, my heart stupid as a lamppost,
waiting for you underneath it every night –

Paper Boats

At the Co-op, all the Valentine cards
have been squashed on their cardboard stand between
the cans of cider and the bleach; a few yards
from the till, bunnies hold roses, lovebirds gleam.

Outside, the sky is full of winter sun,
and I think about the unlikely trick of love
while clouds bloom quietly, become
one thing and then the next, bunching far above,

then drooping over my head. I want to take
each red envelope, fold it into a little boat,
one each, for anyone who has escaped
a sad marriage, or taken a second chance – float

each ship like a lopsided heart, so gently,
sail the yearning we all must carry.

Picking raspberries

The uncertainty of it all. Sometimes I'd find a perfect
pink chandelier, sun-tender, but as soon as I eased it away,
I'd be left with a tiny orgasm of jam that couldn't

wait any longer. Each little body illuminated
with its own fragile nakedness, a soft purple thistle,
absurdity of soft hair, seeds that sewed the tiny

masterpiece together. I imagine what it would be to reach
you, search through scratched years, to undress in daylight,
taste our warmth and heat, that sharp-sweetness of touch.

Kate Fox writes to Mr Splitfoot, New York, 1892

My body made strange things happen. Men would roll fat dollar bills
to sit next to me in the dark, listening for a tap, a crack, then another,
allowing me to translate their dead mothers and wives, my bones
echoing with unbroken messages. I could raise apparitions, liquid
mechanics of make-believe. Now, this whole city is shrunk to the size
of a bottle, a double-tongued devil who makes me thirsty, the knuckles
and joints of this room creak with cold. I dream that I am the cracked
mirror, the rope in the cabinet. Sometimes I laugh at how it all began:
three sisters tying an apple on a string, bumping it along the floor: its
hollow judders enough to frighten and shrink the skin between this
world and the next.

Moderate trousseau

She is buried now, little trusse or bundle,
but watch it backwards – before that,
a widow who does little with her days,
watches cherry trees shiver bright to pink
each spring, as her children become less
distant, skin tautening, beautiful for a while
they start to play again, back to babies, unborn.

Bride and groom step-quick through fountains
of rice that unscatter, reel back to friends' hands,
her going-away dress an unsettled question.
Before that the ceremony: she remembers
putting her white glove back on at the altar,
underseam sewn back again two inches,
wedding ring slipping off softly as lace,
a string of pearls, perhaps, the splendour
and sham of her veil, the light, fragile ivory
of her wedding dress. This way it takes only
a moment to unravel till death do us part –

she steps backwards from the church, out
into sunlight, unclasps her father's arm,
returns her bouquet to its box, where
stems are uncut, unblossom to bud.
Invitations grow blank spaces, envelopes
separate from stamps. A moderate trousseau.
Tea gowns rise from trunk to wardrobe,
china and hankies (a quantity sufficient for
a lifetime) are gathered in receding arms
of aunts and cousins. It becomes lighter yet.
What was his name? For worse, for better.
She is free. Sings in her bedroom. Thinks
nothing of love.

On borders

Northern Ireland, August

They have always grown high here, like hedges in late summer,
burgeoning with blackberried lies – they promise to kiss us with
that sweet sticky heat of home, keep us safe, collect us together –

yet their teeth are bared with briars. *Here* stains heavy, thickening
familiar as rain, an easy hatred to stir up like dust from these
narrow old roads, pavements painted like sad clowns, flags strewn

like razor wire across meek, hungover streets. Our mouths are sewn-up
islands along dark lonely loughs, stayed in the muddied seoch of history:
we are left to imagine *somewhere else,* its open, flickering fields of sunlight.

Miscarriage

It must have been a boy. Ten days late –
        my heart turned to soft coral swaying
in ferocious heat of bath water.

Weighted pain of his quietness, then this –
        sail torn and unstitched, sinking slowly
below my bloodied thighs, blackened

bladderwrack floating across the surface.
        I dredged the fine threads as best I could until
I held a limp curl of seahorse in my hand –

I turned off the bathroom light, lay so still
        on the seabed, hearing each uneasy muscle
of pulse under shallows of my skin, pelvis picked

white, ribbons of flesh floating to feed
        angelfish, bath gritty with salt and sand,
one less pearl to count.

I remember that I, too, have seen
a bat crawl by morning light

Shuffling scrap of unhemmed leather,
broken umbrella, spokes jangling inside her wings,
a surprise of couture dragging dusty along the floor.
She was a charcoal centenarian, coal gargoyle,
fallen so far from the church rafters, almost
unrecognisable with her arthritic limp, tiny
mouse-body hidden by the funeral-circus tents
she was hauling on each side. It disturbed me then,
a creature trying to navigate the world the wrong way up,
an accordion elbowed and twigged, her tiny tarpaulin
awkwardly rigged. I was watching minute defiance
of air and night and myth, the only truth left was her
wheezing shuffle, that shape of slow suffering progress,
inch by inch, creeping towards the wood-rot pew.

All week I have been thinking about the painting, *The Reverend Robert Walker skating on Duddingston Loch*

It has been sleepless and sad, lurching sickness and shame
and I don't know why I keep thinking of the painting,
but all week, I have struggled against its background

muted like winter. In the spare room in the slight hours
I watch a spider spin an invisible line just as the light
begins to branch the sky, air cold as marble;

he skates from carpet to ceiling, his frock coat flowing
as he rises, gliding effortlessly, his body fine black wool,
his elegant legs, elongated from spinnerets, flying

and floating across frozen surface, moving in rhythm
familiar as Leviticus. By five, morning begins
to suggest itself against the back wall behind my bed,

the loch and the Edinburgh hills echoing to me.
I am caught by my sleeping minister – he has taken off
his skates, has come to the end of his sermon of silk.

He is now bunched, weightless nest of a body returned
to a straggle of scrunched legs, hanging just a millimetre
from the ceiling, defying gravity, waiting patiently.

Down here, beneath ice that pushes thick as God's fist
I know I need to start to crawl somehow, soften each blade –

From a distance, a starling looks black

from a distance

I watch you work with such gentle
certainty. An intimacy of wet paint –

a starling looks black, sky-familiar

the rise and fall and shimmer and ooze
of a curved line, beauty of dark meniscus

teach me her true crush of colour

gathered perfectly, folded close as feather.
You balance the edge of a bird's-eye,

how, up close, she is iridescent

supple as 's', smooth as oil, moon-sliver
shrunk to bone-lightness.

her wings unthinkably bright

No peace yet for my animal heart

I suppose the heaviest and lightest things
rest the same when they are buried. A hammock
of earth must ease to sway the low-slung crumble
of soil softly to a glitter of mineral brightness.

Take, for example, the sarcophagus of a horse;
perhaps its eye, the size of a daffodil bulb,
might be the first thing to give itself up,
worms burrowing deep into its dark moon.

I imagine its flesh becoming free, finding
its own rhythm, sinew to seaweed, muscle to tundra,
joint to spindle, a loosening until the flank turns
as wild as the loamy mother who cradles it. I don't

know much about chemistry of decomposition
but I'm learning to carry the heaviest, the lightest
things the same, waiting patiently each year, knowing
what I have buried will come back bright to face me.

Notes

We don't need infinity: A Zokol space suit was used by Helen Sharman during the space flight on board the SOYUZ-TM-12 and MIR spacecraft in May 1991.

Losing Galileo: Britain left the EU Galileo satellite programme following Brexit, 2020.

Ophelia's Head is Finished: Elizabeth Siddal was the model in the painting 'Ophelia' by the Pre-Raphaelite painter John Everett Millais. A talented painter in her own right, Siddall physically suffered as a result of modelling for his painting, lying in cold bath water for long periods of time.

The rest is silence: 'The rest is silence' (Act V, Scene 2) are Hamlet's last words in Shakespeare's Tragedy.

Outrunning the dark: In Irish folklore, the Tuatha de Danann was one of the original tribes of Ireland – that is, until a warrior tribe, the Milesians (or Celts) arrived. The Milesians attacked and won a war against the Tuatha de Danann, eventually driving them underground. Macha is a goddess who is associated with the province of Ulster. According to legend, Macha appears in the form of a young woman at the house of the farmer Cruinniuc. Without speaking, she begins to live and work as his wife, and soon she becomes pregnant by him. When he leaves to attend a feast organised by the king of Ulster, Macha warns him that she will only stay with him if he doesn't speak about her, but he breaks his promise, telling the king that his wife can run faster than his horses. The king orders Cruinniuc to bring his wife to the feast, and makes her race his finest horses. Macha wins the race, but dies after going into early labour with twins (a boy and a girl). As she dies, she curses the men of Ulster to be overcome with weakness, a curse that lasts for generations.

Awaiting trial: In 2017, the Care Quality Commission (CQC) said it was reviewing radiology reporting across the NHS in England after it found that more than 20,000 x-rays had not been reviewed by a radiologist or an appropriately trained clinician at the hospital.

Chardin's woman: Jean Simeon Chardin was an 18th Century French painter, famous for his still life paintings. My poem is inspired by a number of his works, most notably *The Kitchen Maid*, 1738.

Tapetum Lucidum: The tapetum lucidum is a reflective surface that causes the eyes of animals to look like they are glowing in the dark. Many species of nocturnal animals have this layer in their eyes.

Strange creatures: In 1896, Florence Buchanan attended a meeting of the Physiological Society – the first woman to have done so – and some years later she was to become its first female member.

Somewhere over the Rainbow: *The Wonderful Wizard of Oz* is a novel by Frank Baum, first published in 1900.

Taming the wolf (once upon a time): Edward Jenner is considered the founder of vaccinology in the West in 1796, after he inoculated a 13 year-old boy with vaccinia virus (cowpox), and demonstrated immunity to smallpox. In 1798, the first smallpox vaccine was developed. On 8th December 2020, the first person in Britain received the Pfizer Covid vaccine.

Kate Fox writes to Mr Splitfoot, New York, 1892: In the 1800s, the spiritualist movement in America led to many machines and devices to communicate with the dead. Kate Fox – one of the Fox sisters – was a leading figure, and it was believed she and her sisters had special powers. She and her sisters referred to the devil as Mr Splitfoot. She died penniless and an alcoholic in New York, 1892.

Moderate Trousseau: This is a collage poem. Source text: *Etiquette* by Emily Post, published 1922.

I remember that I, too, have seen a bat by daylight: Inspired by Jenny George's 'Threshold Gods'.

Acknowledgements and Thanks

'Awaiting Trial' (published as 'White Coats in Crisis') and 'Galileo' published in *Poets Reading the News*. 'Axe' published in pamphlet *apple, fallen* by Against the Grain Press. 'Bury her softly' and 'cutting back the roses' published in *Flash Fiction Review*: Prose poetry edition. An earlier version of 'Five sleeps till Christmas (Outline)' published by *Black Light Engine Room Press*. 'flower press' published by *Barren Magazine*. 'I remember that I too have seen a bat by daylight' published by *14*. 'Milk Bottle' published by *Ink, Sweat and Tears*. 'Miscarriage' published in pamphlet *A Sky full of strange specimens* by Nine Pens Press. 'M25, Turning' published in *The Result Is What You See Today – Poems About Running* (Smith I Doorstop). 'On Borders' published in Europe edition of *Magma*. 'Yellow Penguin' published in *Amsterdam Quarterly*.

'Paper Boats' commissioned by Poetry on Loan and Birmingham Libraries. 'Silk' was commissioned by Verve Poetry Festival 2022. 'Somewhere over the rainbow' commissioned as part of Coventry City of Culture for BBC Contains Strong Language Festival, 2021.

'Chardin's Woman' won the Welshpool poetry competition 2022. 'Dead Bird' won the Stanza competition on theme of Jazz Winter 2022. 'Kate Fox writes to Mr Splitfoot, New York, 1892' won the Stanza competition on theme of Hauntings, Spring 2023. 'Ophelia's Head is Finished' was commended in the Pre-Raphaelite Society poetry competition 2022. 'Sonnet of swimming parts' was commended in Against the Grain poetry competition 2018. 'Wardrobe' was commended in the Wolves poetry competition 2021.

I would like to thank Jane Commane and Angela Hicken at Nine Arches Press for their dedication, time and attention that brought this book to life. Thank you to the editors of the magazines in which some of these poems have appeared: *Amsterdam Quarterly, Barren Magazine, Black Light Engine Room Press, Ink, Sweat and Tears, Magma, Poets Reading the News, The Result Is What You See Today – Poems About Running* (Smith I Doorstop). I will always be so grateful to Neil Slevin for being the first person to see something in my work and for his insight, brilliance and good humour. Thank you to the Zellig poetry group for their exactitude, expertise and loveliness; to Sarah Doyle,

Ellora Sutton, Sue Burge, Kerry Derbyshire and Claire Walker for their support and poetry sisterhood. Huge thanks to the inimitable Jonathan Davidson who has guided me along the way since letting me enter Room 204. Lucy Tiller and Ed Bankes – thank you so much for your wisdom, generosity and kindness. Esther Dermott – thank you for continuing to be the best big sister in the world. Finally, a debt of gratitude to all my friends and family and to Chris, Olly and Clemmy.